A Guy's Guide to Romantic Gestures

How to Be Romantic and Make a Girl Feel Special

by Jesse Northeimer

Table of Contents

Introduction 1

Chapter 1: Listening Without Underestimating Communication 7

Chapter 2: Remembering (and Celebrating) the Important Things 11

Chapter 3: Paying Attention to Her Needs 15

Chapter 4: Surprising Her with Little Presents 19

Chapter 5: Showing and Expressing Trust 23

Chapter 6: Making Grand Gestures from Time to Time 27

Chapter 7: Acknowledging Her as Your Girlfriend . 31

Chapter 8: Coming Up with Couple Activities 35

Conclusion 39

Introduction

The concept of romance does not come easy to all of us, especially if you're not the kind of person that is naturally romantically-inclined. But even if you're not that good at it, you still want to make your significant other feel special and show your affection for her in a way that matters. It can be daunting and awkward to figure out the right way to do it, but fortunately, this book is designed to provide helpful guidelines as well as specific advice for you to follow.

You need to know right from the start that because we are all different, not everything will work for every woman. So the first thing you need to keep in mind is her personality and the type of girl she is: Is she into obviously romantic stuff, like roses and candy? Or does she prefer subtler gestures? Figuring this out right from the get-go will ensure that you will not go wrong in your attempts to woo her. If you're not sure, start off with a couple smaller gestures of each kind, and gauge her reaction. Soon enough, you'll have a pretty good idea.

It is equally important to remember that not every kind of romantic gesture is appropriate for every occasion. So this will help you learn to discern for yourself which situations call for over-the-top declarations of affection, and which situations you should keep simple and casual.

You should be aware that romantic gestures will certainly help to strengthen a relationship and bring you and your partner closer; but they will only take you so far. This will not mend or rebuild an already broken relationship. Ask yourself if you are trying to be romantic for the right reasons, or if you're trying to do some sort of damage control, making up for transgressions you feel guilty about.

So for the unromantic types who are trying to present their special ladies with displays of affection but are not sure how to go about doing it, this book was written specifically for you. Everyone has romantic potential; one just has to find it and put it to good use for you and your special someone. Let's get started now!

© Copyright 2014 by LCPublifish LLC - All rights reserved.

This document is geared towards providing reliable information in regards to the topic and issue covered. The publication is sold with the idea that the publisher is not required to render accounting, officially permitted, or otherwise, qualified services. If advice is necessary, legal or professional, a practiced individual in the profession should be ordered.

- From a Declaration of Principles which was accepted and approved equally by a Committee of the American Bar Association and a Committee of Publishers and Associations.

In no way is it legal to reproduce, duplicate, or transmit any part of this document in either electronic means or in printed format. Recording of this publication is strictly prohibited and any storage of this document is not allowed unless with written permission from the publisher. All rights reserved.

The information provided herein is stated to be truthful and consistent, in that any liability, in terms of inattention or otherwise, by any usage or abuse of any policies, processes, or directions contained within is solely and completely the responsibility of the recipient reader. Under no circumstances will any legal responsibility or blame be held against the publisher for any reparation, damages, or monetary loss due to the information herein, either directly or indirectly.

Respective authors own all copyrights not held by the publisher.

The information herein is offered for informational purposes solely, and is universal as so. The presentation of the information is without contract or any type of guarantee assurance.

The trademarks that are used are without any consent, and the publication of the trademark is without permission or backing by the trademark owner. All trademarks and brands within this book are for clarifying purposes only and are the owned by the owners themselves, not affiliated with this document.

Chapter 1: Listening Without Underestimating Comunication

Something that is often overlooked by men, but *very* important for women, is listening. You can try to make her feel special in every way you can know how- but the only thing that will truly count in the long run is your willingness to listen. Don't just pretend, or think that if you nod and smile, that will suffice. The simple act of listening to her when she is sharing something with you will count more than any kind of flowers or chocolates or expensive jewelry. This is the ultimate proof of your affection for her and for the importance she has in your life.

Ultimately, it comes down to the respect you have for your significant other. If she is truly important to you, you won't need to make real efforts to remember to really listen when she is talking to you. And I don't just mean listening to her when she's telling you about her day. I'm talking about paying attention to any complaints or dissatisfactions when she expresses them to you, showing that you care and have taken her feelings into account by changing your behavior accordingly. Don't take these as typical female nagging or mean-spirited comments; she is communicating and expects you to respond, either verbally or through practical behavior.

Communication is essential to the well-being of any kind of interpersonal relationship, but is even truer when it comes to couples. Communication goes both ways, and not only it is important to express your feelings and talk to each other about whatever it is that you are feeling or thinking, but also listening and understanding your significant other when they open up to you and try to convey what they are feeling. Don't underestimate the power of good communication and the beneficial effects it can have on your personal connections. Expressing yourself openly and listening to your partner is what romance is all about; you cannot develop any kind of real intimacy without this key element.

This concept stands at the basis of every successful relationship, and while it is not outwardly, explicitly romantic, good communication is something that will be appreciated and cherished by your significant other and is something that will make her feel special, like she is worth something to you. This is ultimately the most important factor when it comes to relationships, because it can make or break your relationship. All the romantic gestures in the world are pointless and ineffective without this foundation of communication; listening, mutual respect, and willingness to understand and take into consideration each other's feelings goes a long way.

Chapter 2: Remembering (and Celebrating) the Important Things

It's not just a cliché that men always forget about birthdays and anniversaries and women get upset over it. Unfortunately, it's the truth! You know when movies depict the type of situation that involve a couple fighting over something like this, and the man ends up having spending the night on the couch? This scenario is definitely inspired from reality. But you can avoid suffering the same fate by following a couple of simple tips.

Taking note of significant occasions and remembering them represents the fact that you care enough about her to pay attention and acknowledge what these days mean *to her*. Not all women will want a big, fancy celebration, but they will all appreciate you knowing when your anniversary is and remembering their birthday. To you, they might be just days on the calendar…but to her, your acknowledgement of them is a symbol of your love and devotion.

Skipping her birthday is one of the worst offenses, because what she will take that to mean that you don't care enough to celebrate her special day, or at least congratulate her on it. You might not like birthdays, and you might not even celebrate your own. But birthdays are occasions that we celebrate socially, and you ignoring hers will deeply hurt her.

Not remembering (or not knowing at all) the date of your anniversary is equally perilous, because she might feel that while she remembers and cherishes that day, or has even given you a small memento to celebrate the occasion, you are not interested enough to do the same, or do not really care about your relationship and the amount of time you have spent together.

The different expectations in a relationship are not that difficult to navigate, and you can learn to make the appropriate acknowledgements and romantic gestures. If you tend to be forgetful, make a point of writing these important dates down. Mark it on your calendar, put in your day planner, and make a note on your phone. Do whatever you have to do to remember.

In addition, it is always a good idea to have something prepared for such an occasion: a gift, a special outing, or a combination of the two. You don't have to go with the traditional flowers, candy and dinner if you two are not that kind of couple. Still, put some effort into preparing something special that you know she will enjoy. It may not be a big deal for you, but it will mean the world to her because you have proved your affection in this way. After all, actions speak louder than words, and preparing something romantic for her birthday or anniversary will undoubtedly greatly please her.

Chapter 3: Paying Attention to Her Needs

This concept goes back to the chapter on listening and communication, and it's all about paying attention. Listening to what she has to say and being attentive to her needs speaks volumes about you, your feelings for her and your relationship. Romance doesn't always have to be flashy, rosy and heart-shaped; romance can consist of letting her eat the last cookie, watching her favorite TV show with her, or running out to the pharmacy to get her cold medicine when she's feeling sick.

Romance can be found in these little every day gestures just as much as it can in the big, obvious ones. Ultimately, taking care of her and her needs is the best proof of affection and devotion you can offer. Grand gestures are meaningless if they are not supported by these tiny snippets of love that you give her every day.

Like anyone else, you will become busy from time to time, and become completely caught up in your own issues. Don't give her the opportunity to feel neglected when this happens. Don't forget to return her calls. Being ignored by the person you love is the worst feeling in the world. So don't ignore her, no matter what other things you may have on your mind. We all crave attention, because we're human beings and this is the way we're wired - so give it to her, because your time and undivided attention are the greatest, most sincere tokens of your love that you are able to give her.

Shutting her out or refusing to share your problems and frustrations will not do you any good; you're not sparing her any unnecessary worry. You're just creating more reasons for it. Let her become more involved in your life, and give her the opportunity to try to help or comfort you in times of trouble. She will love the fact that you trust her in this way, and your connection will grow stronger as a result of this seemingly small gesture.

All this being said, make sure to check in with her from time to time. Paying attention and being there for her doesn't mean contacting her only to go out. Make time to call her during the day just to see what she's up to, or send her a quick text message to let her know you're thinking about her or that you miss her. It's the little things; kind words and constant communication will make her heart flutter and solidify your relationship in the long run.

Chapter 4: Surprising Her with Little Presents

In addition to making sure you remain connected by letting her know how you feel about her from time to time, a good idea can also be to surprise her with presents once in a while. It doesn't have to be on some special occasion, just random. They don't have to be expensive gifts-rather, small tokens of your love for her; a flower, some lipstick, some really good chocolate or any other nick-knacks that you know she likes will send the right message.

It doesn't seem like a lot, but picking something up because it reminded you of her or because you wanted to put a smile on her face is one of the sweetest things you can do and is guaranteed to be much appreciated by her. It makes us all feel special when someone picks something out for us or offers us little presents just because they enjoy spending time with us. Everyone likes to be thought of, and this shows her that she is present in your thoughts even when you are not together and that she is an important part of your life.

The presents don't necessarily have to be of the most romantic sort. You can skip the candy and flowers and instead buy something appropriate for her interests, like tickets to go see her favorite band playing or a gift card at her favorite store, if you know it will make her happy. It can be anything, really, because the gift itself is not the main focus here. What really matters are your kind intentions and the nice gestures you are making for her.

Small demonstrations of attention, like this one, will keep your relationship fresh and the romance alive for a longer period of time. Everyone loves surprises, and the fact that they shake up the routine and add a little bit of excitement to your lives is just a bonus. In fact, it's almost as though they are presents for you too, because seeing the happiness and enthusiasm on her face makes it all worthwhile.

Be careful, however – it's not enough to shower her with gifts if you're lacking in other departments. Don't make it a habit to buy her things in order to make up for some other way in which you are failing her, or as a way to make her forgive your transgressions. Superficial attention given through occasional presents will not repair a damaged relationship. As is the case with all things, moderation and balance are key components for having a successful relationship.

Chapter 5: Showing and Expressing Trust

Regardless of how many gifts you give her and how much they cost, your trust is arguably the most valuable thing you can offer a woman. Trust is one of those factors that is indispensable in a romantic relationship, and opening up to her requires a great deal of confidence in yourself, your relationship, and most importantly, love.

The general consensus is that men tend to keep to themselves and don't enjoy sharing their thoughts or expressing their feelings too much. Now, this is partially because of male nature and partially because of social conditioning…but there are a few more things you can do as a man to show your feelings for the woman you love than letting her in and sharing your every thought with her.

We are all vulnerable when we open up to someone by voicing thoughts and feelings that we've normally kept to ourselves. But it is even harder for men, because of the social conditioning we talked about earlier. Because of this, sharing your secrets, talking about your dreams, your deepest fears and thoughts is a major demonstration of love and trust that you simply cannot replicate any other way.

There is no better way of letting someone know how special they are to you than confiding in them things you have never told anyone else before. A unique connection is created by doing this, and it is one of those rare, deeply personal and intimate gestures you can make toward a person you truly love and have total trust in. You bare your soul to them and effectively make them a co-pilot of sorts when it comes to your secret thoughts and feelings, which is a privilege not many people can enjoy.

Putting your deepest secrets in someone else's hands and making yourself vulnerable to them is no easy task, and certainly is not one everyone will be able to do. But if you work up the courage and decide that it's worth doing, you will be a better man for it. Your bond will grow deeper and stronger, and you and your significant other will be closer than ever before.

It's important to point out that the ability to open up to someone like this requires time and an already-established connection with a very special person. The need and willingness to share your burdens with your significant other appears gradually, over time, after mutual trust has been proven and earned in a variety of situations. However, once you have reached that point, your relationship will evolve to a level of companionship and emotional intimacy that is unparalleled.

Chapter 6: Making Grand Gestures from Time to Time

The grand, over-the-top romantic gestures are advertised everywhere you look for a reason – they work. Now, this doesn't mean that you have to spend your days frantically searching for the next crazy thing you can do to show her you love her. Something like this is not an everyday thing, and you should definitely not skywrite that you love her on her way to work. But doing something out of the ordinary at key moments in your relationship will make her feel like the most special girl in the world and like she has the chance at romance that one only normally sees in the movies.

If you're looking for examples of such slightly eccentric declarations of affection, look no further than romantic comedies. Every crazy thing and all the tricks in the book have already been done and you are bound to get inspired, but if hopping on stage during a concert to tell her you love her or rushing across town to stop her from boarding a plane is not something you see yourself doing, you can limit yourself to less extreme variations.

As I mentioned, these are not the kind of things one does every day, and they are best reserved for occasions that call for them. Doing something like this can be effective when you're trying to "get the girl", as they say. If you're smitten and you've been pursuing her and she doesn't seem to be impressed by your efforts or doesn't think you're serious about it, something big might tip the scales in your favor or give her the push she needs to accept your attention.

Alternatively, proposals are also popular occasions for crazy demonstrations of love. They range from sweet, to public, to downright embarrassing…but answer me this. Which of us has never made a fool of ourselves in the name of love at some point or another? Write a song, make a video, plan a balloon ride or a flash dance routine. But whatever you do, make it count. It is also very important to make sure when planning your stunt that it's the kind of thing she would enjoy or appreciate. If she's a reserved person who keeps to herself, skip the public proposal. If she doesn't like karaoke, maybe avoid singing your love to her onstage. Whatever you choose to do, remember to be sensible about it.

Grand gestures can also be your salvation in a dramatic moment in your relationship, because those do sometimes happen, in real life. If you are currently living in a romantic comedy and she is indeed about to board a plane to fly across the world, out of your life, and you feel like you can't live without her, go after her. There's a saying that goes something like "If you want something you've never had, you have to do something you've never done." In other words, sometimes you need to do crazy things for someone who is worth it, even if that means begging her to stay or boarding that plane to go with her.

Chapter 7: Acknowledging Her as Your Girlfriend

The simple gesture of acknowledging her as your girlfriend may seem simple, stupid and insignificant. But nothing could be further from the truth. Public acknowledgement of your relationship sends a message to her and the people around you that says you are a couple and that this is something that you are proud of and are not afraid to show off. Not doing it might make her feel like you're hiding it, or else ashamed of her and don't want to be seen together in public.

The most obvious move, besides the superficial social media relationship updates, is to take her home to meet your parents. This is an important step, true enough. But if you feel strongly about her, there is no reason not to want her to meet your parents. This unequivocally lets her – and your family – know that you mean business, that she is an important person in your life and special enough that you felt the need to take her home to Mom.

This is not a gesture that is *obviously* romantic, in the obnoxious, over-the-top kind of way, but it is an important step forward in validating you as a couple because you are acknowledging your affection for her and wordlessly declaring your relationship "serious" in front of your family. It is a subtler and more mature sort of display of affection, but one of more substance. And this will help your relationship evolve.

If you're not quite at the meeting-the-family stage yet, introducing her to your friends is another thing you can do to make her feel like she is an important part of your life. There are few things that feel as great as your significant other being proud of you and showing you off to their closest friends. In this way, you again acknowledge her presence in your life and make her a part of your standard existence. Introducing her to the group is symbolic, like a ritual of acceptance and she will appreciate that you made the gesture for her.

Moreover, when you are out in public, don't be afraid to make your connection to her known (albeit without words). Holding her hand as you walk down the street, wrapping an arm around her waist, or kissing her from time to time can seem insignificant, but they make all the difference in the way your relationship is perceived from the outside, or the way she *thinks* it is perceived. I am not advocating being inappropriate in a public setting, but a little PDA never hurt anyone. These gestures are small –but important– signs of love and reassurance and they will make your special lady feel loved and appreciated.

Chapter 8: Coming Up with Couple Activities

I'm sure you know that having time for yourself and your individual hobbies is important. But spending time together is also vital for your relationship to thrive. However, this time doesn't have to be limited to dates; doing things together as a couple can strengthen your relationship significantly. It doesn't have to be anything fancy. Simple activities you would normally do alone will work just fine, but the fact that you include her in these activities will make her feel special.

Invite her over to watch your favorite movie, play video games, or some other such thing you enjoy doing. She might not be the biggest fan of Grand Theft Auto or the Star Trek series, but she will be touched by the fact that you want to involve her and will be pleased by your effort. Alternatively, offer to do something she enjoys, even if it's not necessarily your idea of a good time. I'm not saying you have to play dress-up or get a makeover. But be receptive to her interests and try to appreciate the value she finds in these activities.

Another great thing to do is to try to find a communal hobby or a mutual interest you can bond over and plan to spend time doing together. Hiking together can be very romantic, because nothing says "romance" like being alone together on a mountain. You can also find new experiences to try together for the first time as a couple. Whether it's something as extreme as skydiving, or something as average as bowling, sharing this new experience will make it feel special for the both of you and will remain a fond memory in your lives.

It all comes down to showing interest in her life and spending time together, whatever that may entail. Virtually any activity can become romantic when it is done as a couple, whether it's strip poker or shopping for computer keyboards. Cooking together, walking her dog, browsing at the book store, or even grocery shopping can all become opportunities for bonding and exploring each other's respective tastes and interests.

Conclusion

Relationships are a complicated business, and pleasing the opposite sex can sometimes be a struggle for people. If you're a man with no romantic inclinations, it can be difficult for you to identify this type of behavior and replicate it in your own way without feeling silly or awkward.

Romance can come in all forms. Flowers, candy and serenades do the trick for some women, but they are sometimes less appreciated by others, and herein lies the difficulty. You have to figure out what the woman you are trying to impress would like, and implement your displays of affection accordingly. You might meet a woman who expects the romantic dinner and the public proposal, while another might prefer a subtler shade of romantic behavior, like holding her hand, just being there for her, or introducing her to your parents.

Ultimately, an important lesson to learn is that there is no one-size-fits-all when it comes to romance, because we are all different. We have different expectations and different inter-relationship dynamics. Romantic behavior does not have to be a mystery. It all comes down to showing the woman you care about how you feel, and that can be done in countless ways. They may be more traditional or more unconventional. As long as your heart is in the right place, you can't really go wrong. But that being said, a few words of advice can help, which is why I hereby bestow upon you the gift that is this guide.

This book was written to provide a helping hand and guidelines for the men who think they are fundamentally incapable of romance. Having reached the end of it, I hope you now know that this mentality is not true, and that anyone can be romantic. It requires a bit of insight into the tastes and expectations of your partner, as well a little effort. But most important are the feelings you put into these romantic gestures. Remember- *anyone* can be romantic!

Finally, I'd like to thank you for purchasing this book! If you enjoyed it or found it helpful, I'd greatly appreciate it if you'd take a moment to leave a review on Amazon. Thank you!

Printed in Great Britain
by Amazon